Prayers to Build the Body of Christ

A Prayer Guide as You Pray for Others

La Tanya Simmons-Webb

Prayers to Build the Body of Christ

Published by: Theocentric Publishing Group
                1069A Main Street
                Chipley, Florida 32428

                http://www.theocentricpublishing.com

Library of Congress Control Number: 2014956280

ISBN 9780991481170

"... To make ready a people prepared for the Lord."

Luke 1:17

Acknowledgments

I thank the Lord God Almighty for choosing me to be his child.

I thank the Lord Jesus Christ for his blood sacrifice on the cross and his resurrection that makes it possible for me to live with him forever and ever.

I thank the Holy Spirit for living inside of me to navigate me through this life so that I can be presented to God.

I thank William A. Webb, my husband, for being a godly man, husband and father. His anointed teaching of God's word has helped me better understand the deep things of God.

I thank my wonderful children Torrin and Crystal, Dwayne, Delorean and Kia, and Kameron. I also thank my grandchildren Jackson and Lily. I am thankful for the unconditional love they have all given me.

I thank my parents for introducing me to Jesus Christ at an early age. I thank my mother for teaching me to pray. I thank my father for inspiring me to write this book. He wrote his first book at age 76 (A Special Lillie the life and times of a virtuous woman) and his second one at age 79 (Born near a Manger My life's journey as a first born son).

I thank my brothers, Joe, Stephano and Jimmy and my sisters La Twyla, Shalon, Vina and Traci for being my constant intercessors.

I thank my editor, my daughter, Kameron Webb.

I thank Patricia Campbell for teaching me to pray corporately.

I thank Mary Moore for being my prayer leader.

I thank Aaron Hines, my pastor, who teaches truth and leads by following Jesus Christ, the Messiah.

I thank all of my prayer partners and those who have prayed for me and my family throughout the years. God's answers to your prayers have sustained us.

Foreword

The purpose of this book is to encourage you to pray for family members, friends, co-workers, neighbors or acquaintances who have surrendered their lives to Jesus Christ and for those who have rededicated their lives to him. This book will provide you with prayers to pray on their behalf. It will give you ideas to expand upon.

Many times, we spend hours in prayer for people to come to know Christ as their Savior, and when they do, we stop praying for them. We know that it is just as important to pray for them after they have made this commitment as it was to pray before. However, we often move on and begin to pray fervently for others who are lost, those who don't know God. We should pray for both.

This book is a tool to remind you to pray, for 40 days, for those who have been adopted into the family of God. Ask the Holy Spirit to show you when you should pray, where you should pray and how to pray more effectively for those who are brothers and sisters in Christ Jesus.

As you read through this book for the next 40 days, insert the name or names of your loved ones into the blanks and pray specifically for those individuals.

My prayer is that this book will be used to bring strength to you and to those for whom you pray. Let it be a starting point and a reminder to pray for those who have been saved from eternal death, those who have dedicated their lives to Christ Jesus, the Messiah.

Table of Contents

Day 1 - Thank You Lord for Salvation

Thank you, Father God, for the gift of salvation that has come to _____ through the blood sacrifice of Jesus Christ. Thank you that _____ has been adopted into your family and that he/she is no longer separated from you. Thank you for your mercy and your grace, kindness, goodness and patience in _____ life. Father God, you never stopped pursuing him/her until he/she surrendered to you. Thank you for your love for him/her. Thank you for not giving up until he/she came to know you. You, Oh Lord, are the wonderful and awesome God.

I praise you for opening _____ eyes and ears so that he/she can see and hear you. I praise you, Lord God Almighty, you have helped him/her understand that Jesus died for him/her so that he/she could be saved from eternal death and separation from you. Thank you for helping him/her choose a life with you.

I praise you Lord and thank you that you are willing and able to keep him/her from slipping away. You are able to keep him/her on the path of life that you have charted for him/her. You are able to fulfill the plans that you have for him/her and have had for him/her before he/she was formed in his/her mother's womb.

Lord, you are trustworthy and worthy of all worship and praise. You are able to do all that you have said you would do.

You have made _____ into a new creature, one who will serve you forever and ever. You have placed within him/her every talent and gift that he/she needs in order to be who you have created him/her to be. In this I give you praise.

Thank you Father God, for answering my prayer of salvation for _____ .

It is in the name of Jesus Christ that I pray. Amen.

Therefore, if anyone is in Christ, he is a new creation; the old has gone, the new has come!

2 Corinthians 5:17

Day 2 - Unwaivering Faith

Almighty Lord, you are wonderful. You are just and righteous. You are faithful and true. You, Oh Lord, never change. It is a privilege to be a part of your family. You have given us the ability to please you by giving us faith. Thank you for the gift of faith!

Father God, _____ believes that Jesus is the Christ, the son of God and he/she has faith in you. Thank you for giving him/her the revelation of the truth of the gospel of Christ. We know it is impossible to please you without faith, so I am asking that _____ will always please you by having unwavering faith in you. Each day, help _____ to become more secure in you and strengthen his/her faith.

I know that things will happen that can be disheartening, difficult to digest or outright impossible to process but please do not allow _____ to be shaken. Please help him/her to stand steadfastly in your strength as you take him/her through each obstacle. When things become tough or hard, do not allow his/her faith to waiver.

Father God, do not let him/her doubt that his/her salvation is real. Help him/her know and believe that you are willing and able to see him/her through everything that goes on in his/her life. Holy Spirit, navigate _____ through life so that he/she will know that God is real and has his/her best

4

interest in mind. No thing or person can or will make him/her turn from the Father. Keep him/her on God's path, Holy Spirit.

Now to him who is able to do immeasurably more than all we ask or imagine, according to his power that is at work within us, to him be glory in the church and in Christ Jesus throughout all generations, forever and ever!** I love you Lord God Almighty and I trust you with _____ .

It is in the name of Jesus Christ that I pray. Amen.

**Ephesians 3:20-21

Consider it pure joy, my brothers, whenever you face trials of many kinds, because you know that the testing of your faith develops perseverance. Perseverance must finish its work so that you may be mature and complete, not lacking anything. If any of you lacks wisdom, he should ask God, who gives generously to all without finding fault, and it will be given to him. But when he asks, he must believe and not doubt, because he who doubts is like a wave of the sea, blown and tossed by the wind. That man should not think he will receive anything from the Lord; he is a double-minded man, unstable in all he does.

James 1:2-8

Day 3 - Ability to Worship You Lord

Abba Father, you are worthy of worship from every being and every element in the universe! You are worthy of much more than our highest praise. You are worthy of perfect worship, Almighty God. Teach us to worship you in spirit and in truth.

Holy Father, in order for _____ to begin to worship you in spirit and in truth, he/she has to know who you are. Please allow him/her to know you. Let him/her see your glory, either in the written word, in dreams or visions or in any other way that you would like to reveal yourself. Lord, keep him/her focused on you.

As _____ studies your word, give him/her a greater revelation of your character, goodness, mercy and grace. Help him/her realize that if it had not been for you, nothing would exist. Let him/her hear audibly some of the praise and worship that happens in heaven. Don't allow him/her to be ashamed to worship you here on this earth. Let him/her be free and uninhibited to worship you in spirit and in truth.

Abba Father, you are seeking people who will worship you in spirit and truth, help _____ to be one of those people. Let his/her worship be pure and sincere. Teach him/her your ways; teach him/her to worship you like you desire to be worshiped. Remind him/her to worship you in both the good times and the bad, in the daytime and at night, in the winter and in the summer and forever.

Oh Lord God, how majestic is your name in all the earth.

I pray this prayer in the name of Jesus Christ. Amen.

Yet a time is coming and has now come when the true worshipers will worship the Father in spirit and truth, for they are the kind of worshipers the Father seeks. God is spirit, and his worshipers must worship in spirit and in truth.

John 4:23-24

Day 4 - Knowledge and Understanding of God's Word

Lord God, your word is perfect; Jesus is the Word. Your word is just and powerful, strong and mighty. Your word, Oh Lord, brings freedom and deliverance from everything that would oppress. Your word is truth! Your word is your will. Your word is to be reverenced, meditated upon and loved. Your word is Holy!

Lord God, please show your mercy and grace to _____ by allowing him/her to know and understand your word. Give him/her revelation knowledge of its meaning. Allow it to be correctly recited and taught. Dispel and erase every evil and erroneous interpretation of your word; do not allow it to bring misunderstanding or confusion to _____ or to anyone who tries to teach him/her. Let the true interpretation of your word penetrate his/her heart; let it bring health and healing, correction and discipline, encouragement, strength and truth. I pray your word will not return to you empty, but will accomplish in _____ everything you desire to achieve.

Lord set a guard over _____ lips so that he/she will correctly quote your word.

I pray this prayer in the name of Jesus Christ. Amen.

Your word is a lamp to my feet and a light for my path. Psalm
119:105

Day 5 - Safety and Protection

Father God, you are beyond amazing!! You have all wisdom and knowledge, nothing catches you off guard. You know each trick and scheme of the enemy; you know each weapon that will defeat him. You are the great protector. Abba Father, you are the best father in the universe and you protect your children.

Thank you for protecting _____ and keeping him/her safe. Thank you for not allowing the enemy to defeat him/her. Thank you for not allowing _____ to fall into the enemy's trap. Thank you for providing a way around danger. Keep his/her eyes on you.

Lord God Almighty, help _____ to stay safe all the days of his/her life. Don't allow him/her to do or say things that will bring harm to his/her body, mind or spirit. Protect him/her from those who are jealous, malicious, contrary and hateful. Let _____ see the dangers that lie ahead and steer him/her away from them. Let him/her use godly wisdom to avoid situations and people who would try to destroy him/her. Give him/her wisdom to do your will.

Thank you Abba Father, for all you have done for _____. Thank you for the safety and protection he/she experiences when he/she follows you. Thank you for your love and kindness and your tender mercies. Keep him/her in your way, Lord, keep him/her safe.

I pray in the name of Jesus. Amen.

For he will command his angels concerning you to guard you in all your ways; they will lift you up in their hands, so that you will not strike your foot against a stone.

Psalm 91:11-12

Day 6 - Become a Disciple of the Lord Jesus Christ

Lord God, you are wonderful and magnificent. No one can know you fully because you are so complex and perfect. We get to know you by communicating with you, studying your word and following your commandments. Thank you for who you are. I thank you because you are great. We crave time with you, Lord. When we spend time with you, we become your disciples.

Teach _____ how to become your disciple. Place within his/her heart the desire to become a disciple of the Lord Jesus Christ. Cause him/her to crave the truth of your written word. Bring understanding to its meaning. Provide a place and time for him/her to really learn who you are. Place in _____ path, a godly man/woman to help mentor him/her. Let this person be dedicated to the things of God. Only allow sound doctrine and truth to be taught. Let him/her walk in your ways without compromise. Today when _____ thinks of you, let him/her know that you have prepared someone to walk this journey with him/her. One who is like an accountability partner and teacher. Let their relationship be pure and holy. Introduce these two to each other and help them develop a good bond.

Holy Father, as _____ learns about you, prepare him/her to disciple others as well. Let his/her relationship

12

with you be one that is worthy of teaching others; let his/her walk be a holy one. Father God, guide _____ so that he/she will be your true disciple, one who bears much good fruit.

I pray in the name of Jesus. Amen.

"Come, follow me," Jesus said, "and I will make you fishers of men."

Matthew 4:19

Day 7 - Know Holy Spirit as Guide/Counselor/Comforter

Father, by your design, when a person surrenders his or her life to Jesus Christ, the Holy Spirit comes to live within him or her. Thank you for such a perfect design, a perfect gift. Thank you for giving us a member of the Godhead to live within each follower of Christ. Thank you for not leaving us on our own. Only you Lord, could have devised such a wonderful plan! There is no god like you.

Father God, as _____ learns more about following Jesus Christ and as he/she learns to live, serve, obey and surrender to him daily, you have given him/her Holy Spirit to guide, counsel and comfort along the way. Please let _____ know that this is for his/her good. Holy Spirit is a gift from you, Lord. Help _____ to be sensitive to the voice of Holy Spirit and to listen to his instructions. Let there be a great level of love for Holy Spirit like there is for you and for Jesus.

Holy Spirit let _____ know that you are his/her helper. Let him/her know that you are God too. Let him/her depend on you to receive his/her daily instructions. Change his/her heart so that he/she will be obedient to your will. When a person follows you, Holy Spirit, that person only knows success and victory. Let _____ be victorious in Jesus Christ.

I pray in the name of Jesus Christ of Nazareth. Amen.

But I tell you the truth: It is for your good that I am going away. Unless I go away, the Counselor will not come to you; but if I go, I will send him to you.

John 16:7

Day 8 - Understanding the Gifts of the Holy Spirit

Oh Lord, my Lord, you are greatly to be praised. You have given us everything we need to fulfill your plan for our lives. One thing you have given us is the gift of the Holy Spirit. You have also given to us other spiritual gifts. As I pray for _____ today, I ask that you will give him/her a greater understanding of the gifts you have given to him/her. There are many gifts, and to each of us you give the ones you want us to have. Help _____ understand all of the spiritual gifts you give to your children:

- Interpersonal Gifts—Encouragement, Mercy, Knowledge, Wisdom, Discernment and Giving
- Community Gifts—Teaching, Helps, Leadership, Administration and Apostle
- Sign Gifts—Faith, Healing, Miracles, Prophecy, Tongues and Interpretation

Give _____ a greater understanding of the things of your Spirit. Help him/her use the gifts you have given him/her for your glory.

I pray in the name of Jesus. Amen.

His divine power has given us everything we need for life and godliness through our knowledge of him who called us by his own glory and goodness.

2 Peter 1:3

Day 9 - Embrace Truth, Reject Lies

Lord God, your voice is mighty to save, it is mighty to create, it is mighty to bring correction. Your voice, Oh Lord, is great. The sound of your voice is like the rushing of many mighty waters and you are to be praised and worshiped because of the words you say. Your words are truth!

Father God, I know that every word you say is true. I know that every word the enemy says is a lie. When you make a promise, it will happen. When you utter prophecies through your children, they will come to pass. Every word of the Bible is true.

My prayer for _____ is that he/she will know that whatever you have said is absolute truth. Help him/her to distinguish between your words and the words of the enemy. Do not let there be any confusion as to who has spoken. No person or thing can imitate your voice, Lord. You have said that your sheep know your voice and a stranger they will not follow. _____ is your sheep and he/she will not believe, follow or obey the words or instructions of the enemy, because they are lies. I declare that he/she believes in you and your words.

Thank you Abba Father, for making yourself real to _____ and for letting him/her hear and know your voice.

I pray this prayer in the name of Jesus Christ. Amen.

But they (the Shepherd's sheep)* will never follow a stranger; in fact, they will run away from him because they do not recognize a stranger's voice.

John 10:5

*Parenthesis added.

Day 10 - Put on the Whole Armor of God

Lord God, I pray that _____ will put on the whole armor of God so that when the day of evil comes, he/she may be able to stand his/her ground, and after he/she has done everything, to stand. He/She will stand firm then, with the belt of truth buckled around his/her waist, with the breastplate of righteousness in place, and with his/her feet fitted with the readiness that comes from the gospel of peace. In addition to all this, I pray that _____ will take up the shield of faith, with which he/she can extinguish all the flaming arrows of the evil one. He/She will take the helmet of salvation and the sword of the Spirit, which is the word of God. I pray that _____ will pray in the Spirit on all occasions with all kinds of prayers and requests. With this in mind, he/she will be alert and always keep on praying for all the saints.

I pray in the name of Jesus. Amen.

Ephesians 6:13-18 paraphrased

Day 11 - Ability to Stand and Not Be Moved

Lord God Almighty, what a privilege it will be to dwell in your sanctuary and to live on your holy hill. It will be a joy to gaze upon your face and to dwell in your presence. _____ will have this opportunity because he/she is your child. Thank you for the salvation he/she has because of the blood of Jesus Christ.

I pray that _____ will have a blameless walk before you and that he/she will do what is right.

I pray that he/she will speak truth from his/her heart and that there will be no slander on his/her tongue.

I pray that he/she will do no wrong to his/her neighbor and cast no slur on his/her fellowman.

I pray that _____ will honor those who fear the Lord and will keep his/her oath even when it hurts.

I pray he/she will lend money without excessive interest and will not accept a bribe against the innocent.

Father God, according to your words in Psalm 15: 1-5, everyone who does these things will never be shaken. I pray _____ will never be shaken.

I pray in the name of Jesus Christ. Amen.

Day 12 - Discernment

Father God, thank you for your wisdom. Thank you for allowing us to have free will. Thank you for giving us the ability to make wise decisions. Thank you for all you do for us. Thank you for guiding us into your truths. Thank you for telling us to follow you. Lord God, you are more than we could ever ask for. You are perfect my Lord! Thank you for being our Holy Father.

I pray that you will give _____ discernment today. Help him/her to seek your guidance in every situation. Help him/her to never jump to conclusions, but to always consult you and wait for your answer. When the answer seems obvious, let him/her be cautious and wait for you to give your instructions. Let his/her judgments reflect your wisdom and goodness.

I pray in the name of Jesus Christ. Amen.

Day 13 - Wisdom

To follow your word is wisdom. To obey your command is wisdom. To have no other god except you is wisdom. You are wise Lord God Almighty. It is a privilege to be your servant. Thank you for choosing us.

Father God, I pray _____ will operate in the wisdom that comes from you. I pray he/she will never following his/her own ideas, rules, desires or dreams, but that he/she will always follow you. I pray that every area of his/her life will be steeped in godly wisdom, his/her emotions, finances, intellect, spirituality and physical well being.

Lord God, when _____ doesn't have wisdom, let him/her ask you for it, because you have told us to. You have also said that you would give it to your children who ask.

I pray _____ will speak wise words, pray wise prayers and meditate upon your words; your words are wisdom. Thank you, Father God, for giving us wisdom simply because we have asked for it. Thank you for giving to us abundantly.

I pray this prayer in the name of Jesus. Amen.

Day 14 - Godly People to Fellowship With

Father God, I thank you that in the beginning of time, you fellowshipped with Adam and Eve. You walked in the garden and communed together. What a wonderful time that must have been. Oh Lord, we long to walk that closely to you for all of eternity.

You have told us to assemble ourselves together. When we are obedient to your word, we will be strengthened, corrected and encouraged.

I pray that you will provide a godly person or people for _____ to fellowship with. One or many who are mature and grounded in the truth of your word. I pray they will make time to get together, study your word and talk about the things of this world that can cause people to sin. I pray that they will be accountable first to you and secondly to each other.

Abba Father, it is when we try to navigate this world alone that we sometimes make major mistakes. So, thank you for telling us to get together, build relationships with godly people and minister to each other. We are in the same family with you; you are our Father.

Lord God, when _____ schedule becomes very busy, please let there always be time and energy to meet with whomever you have chosen for him/her to fellowship. Let them meet in a healthy environment, Lord, one that brings glory and honor to you. I pray you will establish lifelong friendships between those to whom you would like to fellowship. They will learn from each other how to better serve you.

I pray in the name of Jesus. Amen

Let us not give up meeting together, as some are in the habit of doing, but let us encourage one another and all the more as you see the Day approaching.

Hebrews 10:25

Day 15 - Being in Christ

Father God, you are the gardener. Jesus is the vine. _____ is a branch on the vine. Father God, you cut off every branch that bears no fruit, while every branch in Jesus that does bear fruit, you prune. The branches you cut off are thrown into eternal fire. They are separated from you for eternity. The branches you prune become more fruitful. Father God, I pray that _____ is a branch that you will prune and that he/she will bear much good fruit, fruit that is pleasing to you.

I pray that _____ will always remain on the vine, Jesus. That he/she will gain his/her strength, direction and victory from Jesus. I pray that he/she will always be a healthy branch as he/she studies and meditates on God's word. I pray he/she will be a strong branch and his/her faith will be strengthened by dwelling in the presence of the Lord. I pray he/she will be very fruitful as he/she obeys your commands and listens to your instructions. Lord, I pray a great harvest will be reaped from _____ branch.

I pray in the name of Jesus. Amen.

John 15:1-17 paraphrased

Day 16 - Desire What God Desires

Father God, you are awesome. You know all things. You do all things well. Everything you allow to happen in our lives, will turn out for our good as we trust you. Your ways are higher than our ways and your thought are higher than our thoughts. Your ways and your thoughts are perfect, Lord. It is a privilege to be your child!

Father God, I pray _____ will desire all that you desire for him/her. I pray he/she will choose the career you want him/her to have, to marry the spouse you would have him/her marry and to live in the house you have chosen for him/her. I pray that every aspect of his/her life will be in line with your desires for him/her.

It is when we follow your ways and your will that we succeed. I pray success for _____. Abba Father, the only way that we can have the same desires for our lives as you have for us is to abide in you and to die to ourselves. When we live in you and you in us, we want the same things. I pray that _____ will turn his/her whole heart to you. That he/she will crave time with you. That he/she will pray and listen to your instructions. That he/she will have an obedient heart and follow you where you take him/her.

I know you desire the best for _____. I pray he/she will desire the best for himself/herself too. You alone are able, Oh Lord, to give to _____ all that you desire him/her to have. Allow your will to be done in his/her live on this earth as your will is done in heaven.

I pray in the name of Jesus. Amen.

Remain in me, and I will remain in you. No branch can bear fruit by itself; it must remain in the vine. Neither can you bear fruit unless you remain in me.

John 15:4

Day 17 - A Prayer From Jesus

My prayer is not for them (the original 12 disciples)* alone. I pray also for those, _____, who will believe in me through their message, that all of them may be one, Father, just as you are in me and I am in you. May they also be in us so that the world may believe that you have sent me. I have given them the glory that you gave me, that they may be one as we are one; I in them and you in me. May they be brought to complete unity to let the world know that you sent me and have loved them as you have loved me.

Father, I want those you have given me to be with me where I am, and to see my glory, the glory you have given me because you loved me before the creation of the world.

Righteous Father, though the world does not know you, I know you, and they know that you have sent me. I have made you known to them, and will continue to make you known in order that the love you have for me may be in them and that I myself may be in them (John 17:20-26). This prayer was prayed by Jesus himself for _____. Amen.

*Parenthesis added.

Day 18 - Physical Health, Healing and Deliverance

Lord God, thank you for being concerned about our spirit, mind, and body. Thank you for making a way for us to be totally set free from death, destruction and sin. Thank you for the blood of Jesus, which makes it possible to live here on this earth in a way that is pleasing to you. Thank you for salvation from eternal death, eternal separation from you, Father.

Lord, I pray excellent health for_____. I pray you will bless him/her with a healthy body so that he/she can fulfill your plan. I pray you will bless his/her mind so that his/her thoughts will be pure toward you and that it will think on things that are pleasing to you. I pray you will bless his/her spirit so that it will commune with you and spend eternity with you. Thank you for the blood of Jesus.

Father God, never let us take the blood of Jesus for granted; what an awesome and holy sacrifice he was in obedience to you so that we could be redeemed and restored unto you. Thank you, Jesus, for your sacrifice. You truly are the Lamb of God.

It is in the name of Jesus I pray. Amen.

But he was pierced for our transgressions, he was crushed for our iniquities; the punishment that brought us peace was upon him, and by his wounds we are healed.

Isaiah 53:5

Day 19 - How to Pray God's Will

Father God, your will is perfect! It is without error! It is mature and complete! It is unchanging!

I pray that _____ will fall so deeply in love with you that he/she will trust you with perfect trust and sincerely pray that your will be done in his/her life on this earth as your will is done in heaven.

I pray in the name of Jesus. Amen.

Your kingdom come, your will be done on earth as it is in heaven.
Matthew 6:10

Day 20 - Live a Holy Life

Lord God you are HOLY. There is nothing corrupt about you. There is no blemish on your record. There is no smudge on your character. There is no slander on your name. You are great and you are greatly to be praised.

We are commanded to live a holy life like you do. Father God, many times we don't know how, but you have sent Jesus to be our example and Holy Spirit to be our guide. As _____ studies your words of truth, help him/her see and understand how he/she is suppose to live. I pray that he/she will put off the old things, behaviors, words and thoughts that are not pleasing to you and put on all that is.

I pray that lying, deception, sexual sin, discord, ferocious anger, harsh words and unkind actions will not be a part of his/her life. I pray that he/she will think, act and talk in ways that bring glory to your name. Abba Father, guide _____ by the Holy Spirit to live a holy life. Help him/her to be quick to repent when he/she has sinned against you. Don't allow him/her to give up but to keep on trying to think, do and say the right things. Let him/her live a life of righteousness, realizing that his/her righteousness comes through the blood of Jesus.

Today, arrest _____ thoughts and turn them to you, Lord. Begin to reveal to him/her your holiness. Amaze him/her with your kindness and goodness. Help him/her imitate Christ.

I pray in the name of Jesus. Amen.

But just as he who called you is holy, so be holy in all you do; for it is written: "Be holy, because I am holy."

1 Peter 1:15-16

Day 21 - Righteousness that Comes Through Jesus

Thank you, Father, for the righteousness that comes to us, through faith in Jesus Christ. Thank you that _____ is considered righteous because of the blood of Jesus Christ. I pray, he/she will never fall away from you or become unrighteous in your sight.

I pray in the name of Jesus Christ. Amen.

But now a righteousness from God, apart from the law, has been make known, to which the Law and the Prophets testify. This righteousness from God comes through faith in Jesus Christ to all who believe.

Romans 3:21-22

Day 22 - Absolute Trust in God

Lord God you are trustworthy, greatly to be praised and worthy of honor and glory. Your name is Truth. You have never let us down. You have never allowed us to go without anything we have needed. Even in the hard times and the lonely times, you have always been there with each of us. You have provided a way of salvation for your children and in that we do trust you with absolute, unwavering and unshakeable trust.

I pray _____ will not be like the people who trust in great wealth, large armies and governments. I pray he/she will be like an olive tree that flourishes in the house of God. I pray he/she will trust in God's unfailing love forever and ever. I pray he/she will praise you forever for what you have done; in your name there is hope, for your name is good. I pray he/she will praise you everywhere he/she goes and that he/she will teach others to do the same.**

Righteous God, when we think of you we are full of praise because if you have said it, it will happen. I pray _____ will put his/her total trust in your word. Your word is truth and it is trustworthy. When _____ cannot see or understand what is happening, let him/her know that you are in control and that you have his/her best interest in mind. Let him/her find comfort in the fact that you never make mistakes. You always do what is right, just and good.

Your name is to be glorified because you are trustworthy, Lord.

I pray in the name of Jesus. Amen.

**Psalm 52:7-9 paraphrased

Day 23 - Never Turn and Fall Away From God

Father God, many people want to dwell with you forever in your sanctuary. They want to live on your holy hill. However, not all who want to dwell with you will be able to. I pray _____ will be one who is with you forever and ever.

I pray that he/she will stand his/her ground even if it involves suffering. If he/she is publicly insulted or persecuted that he/she will not turn from the gospel of the Lord Jesus Christ. Abba Father, if _____ property risks being confiscated or if he/she risks losing all of his/her earthly possessions, I pray he/she will be strong and stand firm on the truth of your word and on the gospel of the Lord Jesus Christ. I pray he/she will never compromise when it comes to you, Lord.

Do not allow _____ to throw away his/her confidence in you; it will be richly rewarded. Help him/her persevere so that when he/she has done the will of God, he/she will receive what has been promised. For in just a very little while, He (Jesus)* who is coming will come and will not delay.** The righteous ones of God will live by faith. If _____ shrinks back from you, then you, Oh Lord, will not be pleased with him/her. I pray you will always be pleased with _____. Keep his/her mind, thoughts, body and spirit turned to you, Lord. Don't allow him/her to be lost forever.

I pray in the name of Jesus. Amen.

But we are not of those who shrink back and are destroyed, but of those who believe and are saved.

Hebrews 10:39

*Parenthesis added.

**Hebrews 10:37

Day 24 - Make Wise Decisions

Lord God, thank you for being the only wise God. Thank you for giving us commands to follow that will guide us and will help us make wise decisions. You have told us in your word to ask for wisdom and you will give it to us. Help us remember to ask for wisdom and to receive it from you.

Holy Father, today I pray for _____ to make wise decisions. That he/she will use wisdom in every area of his/her life. I pray he/she will make wise decisions in relationships, so that he/she will be blessed and encouraged, safe and secure, peaceful and joyful. I pray he/she will make wise decisions about his/her finances so that he/she will use the resources that you have given him/her for your glory. I pray that he/she will give, save and purchase things according to your will. I pray he/she will make wise decisions about using his/her time wisely, remembering to spend time with you in praise and worship, study and meditation of your word. Help him/her use time wisely, and not be wasteful or negligent, but seeking your perfect will for every minute of the day. I pray he/she will make wise decisions about his/her future. That he/she will understand how important his/her future is to you and to the whole body of Christ.

Father God, you are wonderful and you want all of your children to make wise choices. I pray _____ will choose to love and obey you all the days of his/her life.

I pray in the name of Jesus. Amen.

For the Lord gives wisdom, and from his mouth come knowledge and understanding.

Proverbs 2:6

Day 25 - Unconditional Love

Almighty God, you are love. Thank you for being who you are; you are perfect in all your ways. Thank you for loving us and for saving _____ from eternal death and destruction. Thank you for the love and obedience Jesus has for you. Thank you for his blood sacrifice when he died on the cross so that we could be redeemed and restored unto you.

Father God, if we don't have love, then we will sound like noise, we will be nothing and we will gain nothing. I pray for _____ to have perfect, unconditional love like you want us to have. I pray that he/she will receive this same kind of love, agape love, from those whom you have placed in his/her life.

Help him/her to walk in your example of love. I pray _____ love is patient and kind, not envious and not boastful, not proud nor rude nor self-seeking. I pray his/her love is not easily angered and keeps no records of those who have done him/her wrong. I pray it does not delight in evil but rejoices with the truth. Help him/her remember that love always protects, trusts, hopes and perseveres. Love NEVER fails.

I pray _____ will be engulfed by your love today. That he/she will experience your perfect love and that it will be tangible. Thank you for loving _____. You are amazing Holy Father.

I pray in the name of Jesus Christ. Amen.

2 Corinthians 13:1-8 paraphrased

Day 26 - Hope in God, Not the Things of this World

Abba Father, I am so glad you have opened _____ eyes to your truth! I am glad that you have given him/her salvation that comes through the blood of Jesus Christ. I am glad that you have given him/her hope. Thank you that the things of this world don't matter and will not last, but you are eternal, you are forever. Your mercy and grace are great and you, Oh Lord, are greatly to be praised.

I pray _____ will not be consumed or overly concerned by the things of this world, but his/her focus will be on you. I pray he/she will not seek worldly riches or fame, but that he/she will build treasures in heaven where nothing and no one can destroy or steal them. I pray he/she will put his/her hope in you and you alone. I pray he/she will never experience a time when things or activities become more important than spending time with you.

Righteous God, I pray _____ will know and understand what it really means to put his/her hope in you. There are neither worries nor anxieties when we put our hope in you. Let _____ experience your peace.

I pray in the name of Jesus Christ. Amen.

Show me your ways, O Lord, teach me your paths; guide me in your truth and teach me, for you are God my Savior, and my hope is in you all day long.

Psalm 25:4-5

Day 27 - They Will Know Your Name

Father God, those who know your name will trust in you. I pray _____ will know your name. When we know your name, we will know your character. When we know your character, we will put our full trust in you. I pray he/ she will know you as:

- Adonai (ah-doe-NI)—"The Lord My Great Lord" (Psalm 8)
- El (el)—"The Strong One" (Exodus 15:2)
- El Elohe Yisrael (el el-o-HAY yis-raw-ALE)—"God, the God of Israel (Psalm 68:8)
- El Elyon (el EL-yuhn)—"The God Most High" (Daniel 4:34)
- Elohim (el o-HEEM)—"The All-Powerful One" (Genesis 1:1-3)
- Jehovah-Tsidkenu (tsid-KAY-new)—"The Lord is Our Righteousness" (Jeremiah 23:5,6)
- Jehovah-M'kaddesh (me-KA-desh)—"The Lord Who Sanctifies" (Leviticus 20:8)
- Jehovah-Shalom (sha-LOAM)—"The Lord is Peace" (Judges 6:24)
- Jehovah-Shammah (sha-MAH)—"The Lord is Here" (Ezekiel 48:35)
- Jehovah-Rophe (RAW-pha)—"The Lord who Heals" (Exodus 15:26)
- Jehovah-Jireh (YEAR-a)—"The Lord who Provides" (Genesis 22:14)
- Jehovah-Nissi (NEE-see)—"The Lord is My Banner" (Exodus 17:15)

- Jehovah-Rohi (RO-he)—"The Lord is My shepherd" (Psalm 23:1)

When _____ knows you as these names, then he/she will fall deeper in love with you. I pray that this life will not be to hard for him/her because he/she will know your name and he/she will trust in you.

I pray in the name of Jesus. Amen.

Day 28 - Become an Overcomer

Father God, we are on a journey and at the end of this journey, we will have the privilege of being with you forever. We will dwell in your presence and we will be able to gaze upon your face. Each of your children looks forward to the time when we will be with you. In order to live with you for eternity, we must become overcomers. My prayer for _____ is that he/she will become an overcomer.

You have given promises, in your word, for those who over-come. Jesus has promised to each who over comes:

- the right to eat from the tree of life, which is in the para-dise of God,
- they will not be hurt at all by the second death,
- they will be given some of the hidden manna and a white stone with a name written on it, known only to him who receives it,
- they will be given authority over the nations,
- they will also be given the morning star,
- they, like them, be dressed in white. Jesus will never blot out his name from the book of life, but will acknowledge his name before Father God and his angels,
- they will be made a pillar in the temple of my God. Nev-er again will he leave it. Jesus will write on them the name of our God and name of the city of our God, the New Jerusalem. Write on them his new name,
- they will be given the right to sit with him on his throne.

Oh Lord God, what wonderful gifts to those who overcome this world! Please help _____ to become an overcomer so that he/she will dwell with you forever.

I pray in the name of Jesus. Amen.

Revelation 2:7, 11, 17, 26, 28; 3:5, 12, 21 paraphrased

Day 29 - Know God's Promises are True

Your words, Oh Lord, are believable because you have said them. All of your children know that we can depend on your words. We can "take them to the bank". You are the God who does not lie. Every word from your mouth you will fulfill. You have already proven that to us by the blood sacrifice and resurrection of the Lord Jesus Christ. Thank you for your promises.

Lord God, if you have given a promise, then it will happen. It may not happen today or tomorrow or next month, but it will absolutely happen. I pray that _____ will know your promises and he/she will know that they will happen. I pray he/she will not doubt you or your word, but that he/she will have absolute confidence in knowing that what you have said is true and it will come to pass.

Father God, I pray you will speak to _____ and allow him/her to know which promise you are fulfilling in his/her life today. Let him/her see you working things out for his/her good. Let him/her find comfort in you and your promises.

I pray in the name of Jesus Christ. Amen.

For no matter how many promises God has made, they are "Yes" in Christ. And so through him the "Amen" is spoken by us to the glory of God.

2 Corinthians 1:20

Day 30 - Desire to Walk in Obedience to God's Commands

    Abba Father, when a person is in love with someone, they want to do and say things that are pleasing to the one with whom they love. I pray that _____ will fall deeper and deeper in love with you and that he/she will desire to obey your commands.

    You have commanded us to not worry, so I pray he/she will not worry. You have commanded us to have no other gods except you, so I pray you will reveal to him/her the other gods that are in his/her life and that you will help him/her get rid of them. You have told us to love our neighbor like we love ourselves, so I pray that _____ will love his/her neighbor as he/she loves himself/herself.

    I pray _____ will not be consumed with his/her will and desires, but that he/she will follow you and your ways. When you tell him/her something, I pray his/her heart will be turned to you and he/she will obey.

    You have commanded us to not be afraid, so I pray _____ will never be afraid. You have commanded us to trust you, so I pray he/she will have total trust in you. Without faith, we cannot please you, so I pray he/she will have unwavering faith in you. Father God, I know that you only ask us to do what is good for us. Let _____ know that too. Let him/her have a heart of obedience to you Lord.

I pray in the name of Jesus. Amen.

Day 31 - Do Not Grieve the Holy Spirit

I pray that _____ will put off falsehood and speak truthfully to his/her neighbor. I pray in his/her anger he/she will not sin or let the sun go down while he/she is still angry. I pray if there has been any stealing, that there will be no more. I pray he/she will not let any unwholesome talk come out of his/her mouth, but only what is helpful for building others up according to their needs, that it may benefit those who listen. Lord help _____ to never grieve the Holy Spirit. Help him/her get rid of all bitterness, rage and anger, brawling, slander and malice. Teach him/her to be compassionate to others and help him/her forgive just as in Christ God forgave him/her.

I pray _____ will be an imitator of you Lord. If there is a hint of sexual immorality or any kind of impurity or greed, Lord, please remove it from his/her life. These things are not pleasing to you. And you will not allow anyone who does these things to have an inheritance in your kingdom. Also, Lord God, remove any obscenity, foolish talk or coarse joking. Rather let him/her live a life as a child of the light, your Light, Abba Father. Let him/her be clothed in goodness, righteousness and truth.

I pray in the name of Jesus. Amen.

Ephesians 4:25-5:11 paraphrased

Day 32 - Remove Fear, Doubt and Discouragement

Lord God Almighty, when we are in right relationship with you we will not fear, doubt or become discouraged. We will walk in your perfect love. Thank you for the opportunity to walk with you. Thank you for the opportunity to experience your perfect love. Thank you for choosing us to be in your family and placing us under your protection. Thank you for peace, faith and courage.

Abba Father, I pray that where fear, doubt and discouragement may have crept into _____ heart and mind that you will remove it completely. I pray you will dispel all that would come to destroy him/her and all that would come to keep him/her from becoming all that you have planned.

Lord God, you have not given us the spirit of fear, so we know it is from the enemy. I pray _____ will not accept anything from the enemy. Take fear away Lord, and replace it with peace.

Father God, It is not pleasing to you when we doubt you. With you all things are possible. Help _____ remember that your abilities are limitless. Remind him/her of your goodness, strength, power and sovereignty.

Mighty God, you do not want us to become discouraged, so saturate _____ with courage that comes from you. I pray that he/she will go forth in the power and the might of the Lord Jesus Christ to do what you have called him/her to do.

Thank you, Lord, for removing everything that would come to hinder _____. Thank you for placing within him/her everything that will bring victory and success.

I pray in the name of Jesus Christ. Amen.

Scripture reference Nehemiah 5:10-12

Day 33 - Lead Them Not Into Temptation but Deliver Them From Evil

Father God, the world is evil but you are good! There are so many things that will come to distract us and cause us to sin against you. _____ is a follower of Christ. Please alert him/her to the schemes of the enemy. Please let him/her discern danger and turn from it. Cause him/her to walk in your ways all the days of his/her life.

Father God, lead _____ not into temptation but deliver him/her from the evil one.

I pray in the name of Jesus. Amen.

And lead us not into temptation, but deliver us from the evil one.
Matthew 6:13

Day 34 - Give Them Their Daily Bread

Father God, thank you for your promise to give us everything we need. I pray that you will give _____ his/her daily bread. Give him/her everything he/she needs both emotionally, physically, financially, and spiritually. Let there be no lack in his/her life.

I pray in the name of Jesus. Amen.

Give us today our daily bread.

Matthew 6:11

Day 35 - Favor With Both God and Man

Lord God, I pray that _____ will live a life so pleasing to you that you will bless him/her with favor from both God and men.

I pray in the name of Jesus. Amen.

And Jesus grew in wisdom and stature, and in favor with God and men.

Luke 2:52

Day 36 - Repent Often; Forgive Completely

Righteous Father, we sin daily against you. You are so merciful that when we repent, you forgive. Help _____ to be like you.

While _____ is seeking you about how to live a righteous and holy life, help him/her understand that he/she should repent for every offense that he/she has committed against you. Help him/her understand that when someone asks him/her for forgiveness, that he/she should grant it. Remind him/her that even if no one asks for his/her forgiveness, he/she should forgive anyway. Teach him/her to forgive like you do, completely. Lord God, just as we forgive, we are forgiven. Help _____ to forgive the one who has offended him/her, forget the offense and love the person who was offensive.

Jesus taught his disciples to pray "...Forgive us our debts, as we also have forgiven our debtors." When we forgive half way, then that is how we are forgiven. When we forgive completely, we are completely forgiven. Forgive _____ completely for all the things he/she has done wrong and teach him/her your ways.

I pray in the name of Jesus. Amen.

Forgive us our debts, as we also have forgiven our debtors.
Matthew 6:12

Day 37 - Remove Idols

Father God, you are so wonderful. Why do we think we need other gods? When we step back and think about it, you are all we need. You have told us to have no other gods before you. Please help us to be obedient to your command. Reveal to _____ which idol(s) he/she has in his/her life. Please help him/her to love and obey you as his/her God and you alone.

Holy Father, as you search _____ heart, help him/her to be turned totally toward you. Help him/her to not harbor anything or anyone that is not of you. Help him/her repent of serving other things or other people besides you. Help him/her keep his/her focus on you, Lord. If _____ has idols in his/her house, help him/her get rid of them. If he/she has idolized people, help him/her to remember that they are only people; they are fallible and they are not worthy of becoming gods. If he/she has spent too much time thinking about making money, Lord, help him/her keep things in perspective. Please show _____ the need to keep hobbies, activities and other interests in the right order, so that they don't take your place as God. You are all he/she needs and you are God!

Abba Father, I know that _____ loves you and wants to obey your commands. I know he/she has a lot to learn about following you, as we all do. Thank you for sending

Holy Spirit to live within him/her to guide him/her along the way. Thank you for your forgiveness and your mercy. Thank you because you are God and we don't need another.

It is in the name of Jesus that I pray. Amen.

You shall have no other gods before me.

Exodus 20:3

Day 38 - Act Justly, Love Mercy, Walk Humbly With God

Lord God, you are very good and you never require more than we can give. Thank you for being such a merciful and gracious God.

Father God, I pray _____ will give you all that you require of him/her. I pray he/she will act justly and love mercy and walk humbly with you. Please teach him/her how to do each of these things. Help him/her to willingly do all that you require.

I pray in the name of Jesus Christ. Amen.

He has showed you, O man, what is good. And what does the Lord require of you? To act justly and to love mercy and to walk humbly with your God.

Micah 6:8

Day 39 - Rest in God

Find rest, O my soul, in God alone; my hope comes from him. He alone is my rock and my salvation; he is my fortress, I will not be shaken. My salvation and my honor depend on God; he is my rock, my refuge. Trust in him at all times, O people; pour out your hearts to him, for God is our refuge (Psalm 62:5-8).

Father God, I pray th s will be _____ testimony.

I pray in the name of Jesus. Amen.

Day 40 - Go and Make Disciples of All People

Father God, you have given each of us the same command. We desire to obey to you. We know you have put everything within us to make us victorious. Sometimes we don't know how to do what you have asked, but you have given us Holy Spirit to help. Lord, I am praying for _____ to obey your command.

I pray he/she will go and make disciples of all nations, baptizing them in the name of the Father and the Son and of the Holy Spirit, and teaching them to obey everything you have commanded us. When we do this, we know that you will be with us always, even to the very end of the age, because you have promised. You always fulfill your promises.

I pray in the name of Jesus. Amen.

Therefore go and make disciples of all nations, baptizing them in the name of the Father and of the Son and of the Holy Spirit, and teaching them to obey everything I have commanded you. And surely I am with you always, to the very end of the age.
                                                        Matthew 28:19

Epilogue

May the words of my mouth and the meditation of my heart be pleasing in your sight, O LORD, my Rock and my Redeemer.

Psalm 19:14

About the Author

From the time she was born, La Tanya grew up hearing the words of the Bible in a Christian household and Spirit filled churches. She has witnessed prayers answered by the Lord God Almighty. At the age of four, she asked Jesus to be her Savior.

La Tanya has learned to trust God in every area of her life. She and her husband William have four wonderful children, two grand children, and have been blessed with a great daughter-in-law and son-in-law. She and her husband now reside in Southern Alabama.

To order books or schedule a speaking engagement, email La Tanya at prayerstobuildthebody@yahoo.com